Southern Lot[...]

# GIRL SPACES

## CUTE & EASY COLORING BOOK

# COLORING

## LET YOUR IMAGINATION RUN WILD!

Coloring takes us to a world where (freedom,) (creativity,) and (self-expression) really pop, giving us a fun break from all the modern-day stress. It has not just become a relaxing activity but a must-have in our daily routine.

## ------- SHARE WITH US! -------

Your unique style makes every coloring page special. We'd (love) to see (your creations!) Drop some pictures with your feedback so we can enjoy the awesome work of a creative artist like (you!)

scan to join with us!

Southern Lotus

## CONNECT WITH US

Please feel free to reach out to us if you have any questions.
coloring@southernlotus.com

# 1000+

## FREE DIGITAL COLORING PAGES!
### Grateful for your choice!

Scan the QR code
for free digital pages

Southern
Lotus

## Share your masterpieces with us.
## Always look forward to your amazing creativity

@southernlotus.publishing

Southern Lotus Coloring Book

@southernlotus_publishing

@southernlotus.publishing

@southernlotus.publishing

@southernlotuscoloring

# CONNECT, SHARE and LEARN

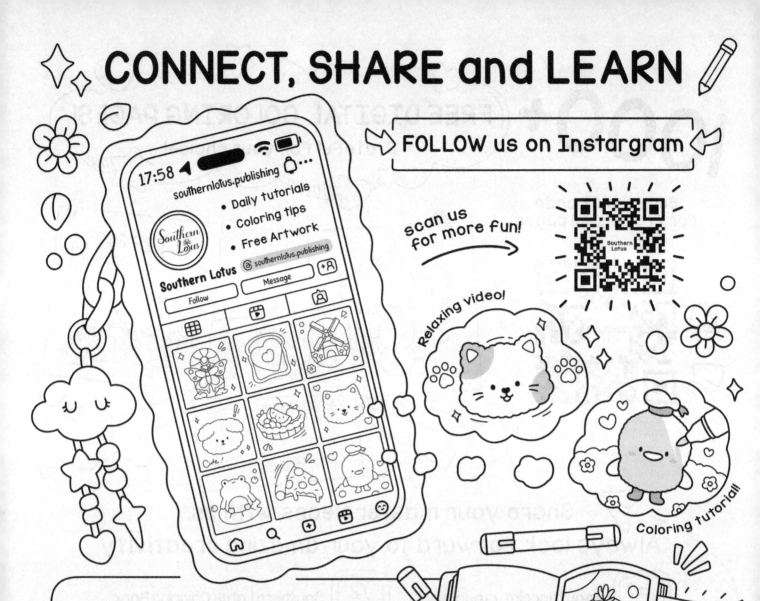

**FOLLOW us on Instargram**

17:58

southernlotus.publishing

- Daily tutorials
- Coloring tips
- Free Artwork

Southern Lotus

southernlotus-publishing

Southern Lotus

Follow    Message    +A

scan us
for more fun!

Southern Lotus

Relaxing video!

Coloring tutorial!

## A LITTLE NOTE BEFORE COLORING!

We select standard-quality paper to keep our products affordable due to the limited options available on Amazon. If you experience bleeding with certain pens or markers, placing a blank sheet of thicker paper behind the page can help. We are grateful for your understanding.

blank paper

THIS BOOK BELONGS TO

# TEST COLOR PAGE

# TEST COLOR PAGE

Use this paper underneath to prevent ink seepage and maintain the integrity of your creation (Optional)

# BOLD AND EASY COLLECTION

Made in United States
Orlando, FL
12 December 2024

55483621R00052